I Wonder Why

Soap Makes Bubbles

and Other Questions About Science

Barbara Taylor

KINGFISHER

KINGFISHER
Kingfisher Publications Plc
New Penderel House, 283-288 High Holborn,
London WC1V 7HZ

First published by Kingfisher Publications Plc 1994
(hb) 10 9 8 7 6 5 4 3 2
(pb) 10 9 8 7 6 5

A CIP catalogue record for this book
is available from the British Library

ISBN 1 85697 227 5 (hb)
     1 85697 228 3 (pb)

Phototypeset by Tradespools Ltd, Frome, Somerset
Printed and bound in Taiwan

Series editor: Jackie Gaff
Series designer: David West Children's Books
Author: Barbara Taylor
Consultants: Ian Graham; Geoff Puplett
Editor: Claire Llewellyn
Art editor: Christina Fraser
Cover illustrations: Ruby Green, cartoons by Tony Kenyon
   (B.L. Kearley)
Illustrations: Chris Forsey 6-7m/tr, 9br, 12-13, 14-15,
   21tr, 23 tr/br, 24-25, 27tr, 28-29, 30-31; Ruby
   Green 4-5, 7br, 8-9bl/m, 16-17, 22-23m, 26-27m;
   Biz Hull (Artist Partners Limited) 10-11m, 18-19m,
   20-21m; Tony Kenyon (B.L. Kearley) all cartoons

CONTENTS

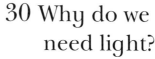

What is science about?

Science is all about discovering how and why things happen in the world around you. It's about everyday things like finding out where water goes when it boils, as well as more complicated things like why we need water to live.

3 Put some water in the freezer and leave it for an hour or two. What do you notice when you take it out? The water isn't liquid any more – it's a solid, and you can't pour solids.

2 Now fill a jug with water and pour it into a cup. Most liquids will pour, but some move faster than others. Try pouring some honey into a saucer – does it move as quickly as water?

1 The kitchen is a great place for scientists. Start by turning on a tap and looking at the water that flows out. Runny things like water are called liquids.

4

What do scientists do?

One of the first things scientists do is to ask questions. Then they try to answer the questions by looking closely at things and testing out their ideas. We call this experimenting. Scientists sometimes manage to come up with the answers – but not always!

4 All liquids can change shape, but most solids can't. Pour some water into a jelly mould and it will fill up all the nooks and crannies. What happens when you put ice cubes in?

5 Ask a grown-up to put a cup of water into a saucepan and boil it for you for 5 minutes. Lots of steam comes off, doesn't it? Let the water cool, then pour it back into the cup. There's less water now – where has the rest gone?

6 When water boils, it changes from a liquid into a gas called water vapour. We can't see this gas, so it looks as though the water has disappeared.

5

What can walk on water?

Tiny insects called pond-skaters are so light that they can walk across water without sinking into it! But even pond-skaters wouldn't get anywhere without a force called surface tension. This pulls on the surface of the water, making a thin stretchy 'skin' on the top.

● Raindrops aren't quite round – they're almost flat underneath.

Why are water droplets round?

Small drops of water are almost perfectly round because they are pulled into this shape by surface tension. Bigger drops spread out, though – they're too heavy for surface tension to work so well.

● The Jesus Christ lizard runs so fast that it can cross rivers and lakes without sinking – a brilliant way to escape from danger!

● Gently touch a drop of water with a soapy straw, and see how the drop gets flatter. This is because soap weakens the surface tension of water – it can no longer pull the drop into a neat round shape.

Why does soap make bubbles?

Adding soap to water weakens the pull of the surface tension, and makes the surface of the water much stretchier. It spreads out enough for you to blow air inside – it's a bit like blowing up balloons with water.

Why do armbands help me to float?

When you blow up your armbands, you push lots of air inside them. Air is much lighter than water, so it helps you to float. But the water helps, too, because it pushes up on things. By pushing up on your armbands, it keeps you floating on the surface.

● Armbands help to keep you safe while you're learning to swim. The air inside them stops you sinking.

● It's easier to float in salty sea water than in fresh water. The Dead Sea in the Middle East is the world's saltiest sea – swimmers can't sink in it, even without armbands!

● Experiment with floating and sinking by finding five things that are light enough to float, and five that sink because they are too heavy.

8

● Divers don't want to float. To help them sink, they wear a belt with heavy weights on it – not something you should try!

● Many fish have a bag of air called a swim bladder inside them. It works a bit like an armband. When fish fill the bladder with air, they float high in the water. When they let the air out, they float lower down.

Why do sharks have to keep swimming?

If sharks stop swimming they sink like stones. This is because they are heavy for their size, and they don't have swim bladders. They have to keep swimming to stay up in the sea, just like you have to swim or tread water.

Why do I run out of energy?

● When you run, the stored energy in your body is changed into movement energy.

You run out of energy because you use it! Walking, running and jumping all need energy – without it you wouldn't be able to talk, write, read or even sleep! Energy is stored inside your body and comes from your food. That's why you get hungry – your body is telling you to put back some of the energy you've used.

● Lots of things give out energy, in many different forms. Here are just some of them.

Fire = heat energy

Bike = movement energy

Drum = sound energy

● Eating a small apple gives you enough energy to sleep for half an hour.

● Energy is never made or destroyed. It just changes from one form to another. Bending a bow stores energy in the bow. This changes into movement energy as the arrow flies from the bow.

What is energy?

Energy makes things happen – nothing in the universe would work without it. You can't see energy, but you can see what it does to things around you. Because of energy, cars move and planes fly, lamps give out light, drums make music, and fires give off heat.

Food = chemical energy

Train = electrical energy

Torch = light energy

Why does the spoon get hot when I stir my cocoa?

Heat energy never stays still. It is always moving. The teaspoon warms up when you stir your cocoa because heat energy is moving from the hot drink into the spoon.

● Things that allow heat to pass through them easily are called conductors. A metal spoon is a good conductor.

● Our bodies give off heat all the time. Some burglar alarms work by picking up the heat given off by a burglar's body.

Why is sunlight warm?

Sunlight is warm because the Sun gives off heat as well as light energy. The Sun's heat energy travels towards us in invisible straight lines called heat rays. You can't see them, of course, but you can feel them on your skin on hot sunny days.

- You get cold feet when you stand on a tiled floor because the tiles carry heat energy away from them. Your feet feel warmer on a carpet because it doesn't carry heat away as well as the tiles do.

How do hang-gliders hitch lifts?

When the Sun heats the land, the land then warms the air above it. Warm air is lighter than cold air, and it rises up into the sky. Hang-gliders use this rising warm air to help them to fly. The rising currents of warm air are called thermals.

How do divers keep warm?

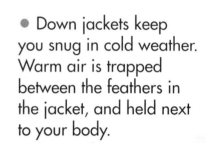

The problem with heat energy moving about is that it sometimes makes it difficult to keep warm. Divers often wear rubber wetsuits in cold water because rubber doesn't conduct heat well – it stops body heat from escaping as quickly as it would normally. Things that don't carry heat energy well are called insulators.

● Down jackets keep you snug in cold weather. Warm air is trapped between the feathers in the jacket, and held next to your body.

● Beneath their skin, seals have a thick layer of fat called blubber. This insulates their bodies and helps to keep them warm in the coldest seas.

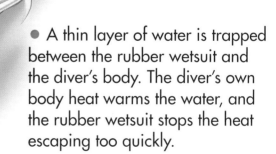

● A thin layer of water is trapped between the rubber wetsuit and the diver's body. The diver's own body heat warms the water, and the rubber wetsuit stops the heat escaping too quickly.

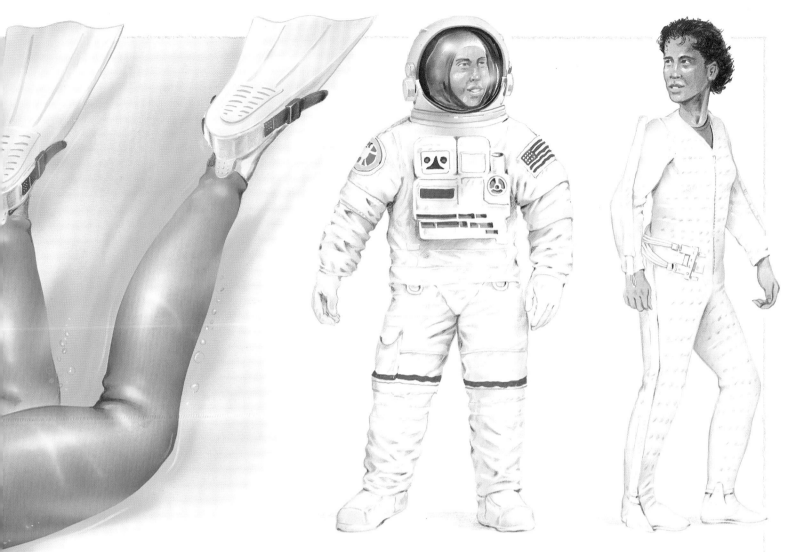

• The Space Shuttle needs to stay cool, too! Special tiles insulate the Shuttle and stop it getting too hot.

• Saucepan handles are made of good insulators. If they weren't, they'd get too hot and burn your hand!

How do astronauts keep cool?

The Sun's rays are much stronger out in space, so astronauts need special ways of keeping cool. Under their spacesuits, they wear a suit of stretchy underwear, a bit like long johns. Tiny plastic tubes run through the under-wear, carrying cool water. The water takes away the astronauts' body heat, and helps to keep them cool.

Why do I feel cold after a shower?

Your body is always giving out heat. When you're wet, your body heat turns some of the water on your skin into the gas water vapour. This change from a liquid to a gas is called evaporation.

You begin to feel shivery after a shower because evaporation uses up heat.

● When you dry your hair with a hair drier, you are heating the water in your hair until it evaporates.

What makes bathroom mirrors fog up?

After a shower, the air in the bathroom is warm and steamy. When it hits a cold surface such as a mirror, the air cools down and changes back into tiny water droplets. These then fog up the mirror. The change from a gas into a liquid is called condensation.

● After a chilly night, you may see tiny drops of dew sparkling on spiders' webs or grass. Dew comes from water vapour in the air. If air cools down enough during the night, water vapour condenses to form dew.

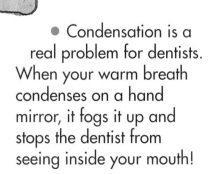

● Condensation is a real problem for dentists. When your warm breath condenses on a hand mirror, it fogs it up and stops the dentist from seeing inside your mouth!

What is sound?

Sound is a type of energy. It happens when something shakes or moves back and forwards really quickly. The shaking movements are called vibrations. You hear sounds because vibrations travel through the air into your ears.

● Some singers can sing a note which is so high and so loud that it breaks a glass!

● Here's a way to see how sounds vibrate. Tie a piece of thread to some tissue paper. Now, put on some loud music and hold the thread in front of a loud-speaker. The vibrations should make the tissue paper shake. If they don't, turn up the music!

● Crashing a pair of cymbals together makes them vibrate, sending out ringing sounds.

Why do trumpeters blow raspberries?

Blowing raspberries is the only way to get sounds out of a trumpet! It makes a trumpeter's lips vibrate, and this makes the air inside the trumpet shake, too. The air comes out the other end as a musical note!

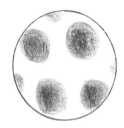

● Sound travels through air at 340 metres per second. That's nearly the length of four football pitches.

Can sound travel under water?

● Sound needs something to travel through – air, water, or some other material. There's no air in space, so astronauts have to use radios to talk to one another.

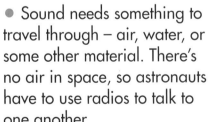

Yes, it can! Sound moves four times faster through water than through air. It can travel such long distances that whales can hear each other when they are over a hundred kilometres apart.

Why do shadows happen?

Light travels in straight lines called rays. When the rays hit something that they can't shine through, the light is blocked, and a dark shadow forms on the other side.

• There are lots of things that light can't shine through – walls, furniture, your own body, for example. We call these things opaque.

• Try to make animal shadows on a wall by wiggling your fingers in the beam of a bright torch.

• Light is another kind of energy. Plants use the energy in sunlight to make food for themselves in their leaves. Sunflowers get all the sunlight they can by turning to face the Sun as it moves across the sky.

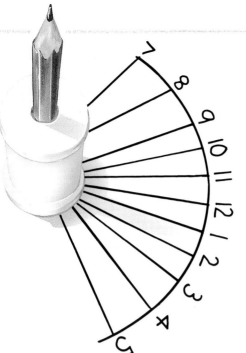

- Did you know that you can use shadows to tell the time? Next time it's sunny, stand a pencil inside a cotton reel on a piece of paper. Every hour, draw a line along the pencil's shadow, and write down the time. Now you can use your shadow clock to tell the time on every sunny day.

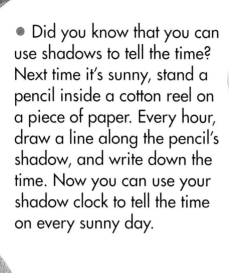

Why can I see through glass?

You can see through glass because it's transparent – that means it's clear, and it lets the light shine through. Glass is great for windows because it lets sunlight into a room, and allows you to see what's going on in the world outside!

- Bathroom windows are often made of frosted glass. This still lets some light through, but the frosting stops people from seeing straight through the glass.

Can light bounce?

When rays of light hit something that they can't shine through, they bounce off it – just like a ball bouncing off the ground. This is called reflection. We are able to see things because light is reflected off them into our eyes.

● You can see yourself when you look down into a puddle because the smooth water reflects the light straight back into your eyes.

● Up periscope! A submarine officer looks through a periscope to see what's happening above the water. Mirrors inside the periscope reflect light from things above the water straight down into the officer's eyes.

● The Moon reflects light from the Sun. It has no light of its own.

● See what happens when light passes through a single drop of water. Cut a hole in a piece of card and stick clear tape over the top. Carefully put a drop of water on the tape and look through it at something small, like a ladybird. It will make it look bigger.

Why do my legs look shorter under water?

When light enters water, its rays travel more slowly than they do through the air. This changes the way we see things. Looking down through the water in a swimming pool, your legs look very short and dumpy. Don't worry – they aren't really!

● As light passes through water, it changes the way we see things. This makes it tricky to net fish – they aren't where they appear to be. To catch one, you have to aim below the place where you actually see it.

Why do rainbows happen?

Although sunlight looks white, it's really made up of lots of different colours. During a shower of rain, the Sun sometimes shines through the tiny raindrops that fall through the air. When this happens, the water makes the light spread into all its different colours. The colours always appear in the same order, and a beautiful rainbow forms in the sky.

Card   Torch beam

Reflected light

Mirror

● Another way to see a rainbow is to hold a mirror in a shallow dish of water. Try to bounce sunlight or torchlight off the mirror on to a piece of white card. The water should make the light spread out into a rainbow.

● You don't have to wait for rain to see a rainbow. Water the garden on a sunny day, and you may see rainbow colours in the spray.

Why is grass green?

We see things when light reflects off them into our eyes. But not all of white light's colours are reflected. Some are soaked up. Grass looks green because it soaks up all the colours in white light apart from green.

● The bright colours of many animals often work as a warning. The black and yellow stripes on a wasp warn us – and other animals – to keep away from its poisonous sting.

Can cats see in colour?

● Many animals don't really need to see in colour. They rely far more on their sharp hearing and sense of smell.

Yes, they can – but they don't see all the colours that you do! Cats don't really need to see bright colours, as most of them are busiest at night, outdoors hunting for food.

What is air made of?

Air is a mixture of gases – mostly nitrogen and oxygen, with a little bit of carbon dioxide and some water vapour. It also has tiny bits of salt, dust and dirt. You can't see, smell or taste the air, but you can feel it when the wind blows.

● You're using air when you take a deep breath and blow out the candles on a cake!

● We don't notice it, but the air around us is heavy, and pushes down on us. The air in a medium-sized room weighs as much as 70 cans of baked beans!

How do bubbles get into fizzy drinks?

The bubbles in fizzy drinks are made of carbon dioxide. The gas is squashed into the bottle so hard that it disappears into the drink. When the bottle is opened, the bubbles have room to escape and start fizzing into the air.

● Make your own bubbles of carbon dioxide gas by adding a teaspoon of baking powder to a beaker of water. Stand by for the fizz!

Why do cakes rise?

When you put a cake in the oven, the mixture heats up and makes bubbles of carbon dioxide. These grow bigger in the heat, and make the cake rise.

● The air you beat into a cake mixture also helps to make the cake deliciously light.

Why do bikes have tyres?

Tyres help a bike to grip the road safely. Look closely at a tyre, and you will see that it is patterned. This pattern is called the tread. In wet weather, water escapes from under the tyre through grooves in the tread, stopping your bike from skidding.

● As a tyre rolls along, it rubs against the road. This rubbing creates a slowing force called friction, which helps the tyres grip.

Why are tyres full of air?

Pumping air into bicycle tyres makes them springy. They are like a cushion between the wheel and the road, rolling easily over all the bumps, and giving you a much comfier ride.

How do bike brakes work?

When you squeeze your bike's brake levers, brake pads scissor in and grip each wheel. The pads and wheels rub against each other, making friction which slows the wheels down. Squeeze the levers tightly, and your bike will stop completely!

Brake pad

Brake pad

Tread

● Without friction, we would slip over every time we tried to walk! It would be like sliding on banana skins the whole time.

● It's hard work pumping up a tyre. You have to squash lots of air into a very small space.

Why do we need air?

All the animals on Earth need to breathe the oxygen in air to stay alive – and that includes you! That's because bodies use oxygen to make energy for living and growing.

● All plants need air, light and water to live and grow. So do people, and every other living thing on our planet.

● Even though they live in the sea, whales breathe oxygen from the air. Sperm whales can hold their breath for up to two hours before coming up for air.

Why do we need light?

Without the Sun's light, there would be nothing to eat! Plants are the only living things that can make their own food, and they need sunlight to do this. Everything else on Earth feeds on plants, or on plant-eating animals. If there weren't any plants, we'd all starve to death!

● If you've ever been camping, you'll know that the grass beneath a tent goes pale and begins to die. This is because it can't get the sunlight it needs to stay alive. Don't worry, it soon recovers!

Why do we need water?

It's hard to imagine, but more than two-thirds of your body is made of water. And the same is true for most other animals and plants. All of the living things on Earth need water to stay alive. Without it, they would die.

● You can survive for many weeks without food. But without water you'd last just three or four days.

Index